TOP SECRET in the WESTCOUNTRY until NOW!?

Published by:

Shark Cornwall Publishing, 20 Dean Clarke House,
Southernhay, Exeter, EX1 1AP.
First published 2023
©Richard Peirce, Shark Cornwall Publishing
ISBN no. 978 – 1 -7395306 – 2 - 4
Photographs: Richard Peirce, Shutterstock and other non-copyright internet sources, our apologies if in error we have breached any copyrights
Layout and Design: Michelle Panter
Printed by Booths Print, The Praze, Penryn, Cornwall, TR10 8AA

BY THE SAME AUTHOR

Pirates of Devon & Cornwall
Execution Sites in Devon & Cornwall
West Country Witches, Wizards & Warlocks
Sharks in British Seas
Sharks off Cornwall & Devon
U.K. Great White Shark Enigma
Shark Attack Britain
The Poachers Moon
Giant Steps
Nicole
Cuddle Me, Kill Me
Orca
Pangolins, Scales of Injustice
Kalahari Gold
A Kalahari Cocktail
Westcountry Outlaws, Highwaymen & Rogues
50 Westcountry Heroes, Villains & Famous Characters

Dedication

This book is dedicated to all those in the U.K.'s security & intelligence services who work tirelessly to keep the country safe.

Richard

Thanks & Acknowledgements

Carl Ahmed
John Burrow
Andrew Chatterton (author)
Sam Coley
Captain John Davison
Devon Live
Dragonfly Films Ltd
Sqeez D'Souza
Matt Everett
Google
Martin Hemmerle
Ray Hopgood
Arthur Madge
Hugh Monro
Michelle Panter
Jacqui Peirce
Perry Richardson
Chris Pringle
Clare Roberts
Angela Tate
Len Tozer
Kate Werran (author)
Tim Whittard
Wikipedia

TOP SECRET in the WESTCOUNTRY until NOW!?

I hope readers will find this a fun and informative read, the title should not be taken too literally! Who can resist a secret or a spy story? Anyone who is told a secret will almost certainly not be able to resist telling at least one other trusted person, and due to this it is easy to see why no secret remains a secret for long!

Those who possess a secret about what is going on around them which others don't possess will often feel slightly superior. Knowledge is power and knowledge of secrets is not only powerful it has sometimes influenced the fate of nations.

James Bond is an action hero who gets beautiful women, drives fast cars and plays with amazing gadgets. His character is loosely based on a retired naval officer who joined the UK's Foreign Intelligence Service – MI6. The films draw their audiences due to Bond's action hero appeal, but look at the shelves of any bookshop and you will see that books about real secret agents and spies are one of the genres that never lose their popular appeal. Why is this? It is because we all love the idea of something secret.

Contents

Introduction

This is the sixth book in what we call our 'black book series'. I have long been fascinated by the idea that Westcountry locals and visitors are often living on top of, or travelling past, places where things happened which they have no knowledge of. This idea was the basis of *Execution Sites in Devon & Cornwall* which was my second 'black book', and also of my *Outlaws and Highwaymen* book. Devon and Cornwall are home to countless past and present secrets. How many visitors relaxing and swimming on Crooklet's Beach in Bude know that under the sands and going out to sea from the beach and across the Atlantic is a fibre optic cable which could be a prime target for an enemy in time of war? There are lots of different types of secrets from tittle-tattle to state secrets, which are covered in the UK by the Official Secrets Act.

Is there a massive intelligence gathering centre in North Cornwall, was there ever a real Beast of Bodmin Moor, and if so was its presence covered up? When Dr. Beeching closed lots of local railways in the 1960's why was the track from Taunton to Minehead left there and maintained? Are Cornish people exempt from paying tax to the UK Chancellor of the Exchequer? These are all interesting questions that are not often asked because very few people are aware of them. This book is not intended to be an explosive expose of previously hidden facts. I wrote it because I believe that many of the stories are interesting, some are worrying and others are good fun, it is not all to be taken too seriously!

Not everyone is interested in baring their all, so I am sure that while nearly half of the UK's most popular nudist beaches being in Devon & Cornwall is not a secret, it is not something that is common knowledge either. Those who do bare all may try to keep the locations of the nudist beaches secret, but of course once they are on the beach, there are no secrets!

ONE

The Madness of War

Towards the end of World War Two thousands of United States service personnel were in Britain preparing for the D-Day landings and the liberation of Europe from Nazi rule. On Sunday September 26th 1943 in the normally quiet Cornish town of Launceston a bizarre, now largely forgotten, shooting incident took place between black and white American soldiers in the town square.

One aspect of the madness of war in those days was that although black and white soldiers would storm Normandy's beaches together, and fight and die together, when it came to eating, drinking, accommodation and training etc., black and white troops were segregated. Institutional racism still reigned in the armed forces of the United States, and in Britain this was very evident in the many places around the country where large numbers of US service personnel were stationed. The shooting incident was widely covered in the tabloid press in Britain and the US under headlines screaming about 'Shootouts' and 'Wild West Mutiny' etc. Apart from the excitement of a Wild West shootout, public interest in Britain was further stirred because the incident was all about race, it was white versus black. At any one time there were over one and a half million US servicemen in Britain, and approximately one hundred and thirty thousand of these would be black. The British were mostly bemused by the tensions between black and white American soldiers, and the often insulting and demeaning treatment they witnessed black soldiers being subjected to by their white "comrades in arms".

If anything most Britons sided with the black soldiers, and disapproved of the treatment meted out to them by the white MPs and officers.

In Launceston simmering tensions boiled over when a large number of black soldiers had suddenly had enough of insulting and discriminatory treatment. White military police had been ordering blacks out of pubs and dances in the town and stopping them going into these places when they could. On the fateful Sunday 40 – 50 black soldiers left the town and marched back to their camp at Pennygillam. There they armed themselves with rifles and automatic weapons before trooping back into the town to forcefully protest against their treatment. In the market square near to The White Hart Hotel at about 10.30 pm they were confronted by white US army MPs and other white American soldiers. Witnesses said the tension in the air was almost tangible, and soon shots rang out. The black GIs had opened fire, and as a result two white military police sergeants were wounded in their legs. There was chaos as British soldiers, civilians, Land Army girls and Americans all scrambled for cover.

It was all over in about five minutes when the firing ceased, and the shooters disappeared into the darkness. The incident was certainly more of a protest than a calculated attempt to injure or take life. A large number of shots were fired and shop windows were shattered. Two army jeeps were riddled with bullet holes, and in various places around the square there were gouges and holes made by bullets.

A few days later fourteen black soldiers from the 58th 1st Ordnance Ammunition Company were on trial in Paignton facing Court Martial charges. All fourteen men pleaded not guilty to various charges, but in what many claim was a rigged trial all fourteen were found guilty. In an almost unprecedented step the verdicts and the fate of the men fell into the SECRET category, because the outcome was censored by the Court Martial President and not revealed publicly. There was speculation that the fourteen black GIs had been executed in England, or that they had been deported.

It would take seventy-seven years for the truth to come out which happened when author Kate Werran's excellent book – *An American Uprising in Second World War England, Mutiny in the Duchy* – was published in 2020. Werran's thorough investigative work confirmed that the results of the trial had been kept secret, but she revealed that all fourteen men had been dishonourably discharged and given disproportionately harsh sentences, sentences that today would be regarded as ludicrous. Eleven were sentenced to fifteen years hard labour, and the other three to twenty-five years hard labour. The last and only photograph of the fourteen accused was a snapshot of them smiling and smoking cigarettes after leaving Paignton police station before they climbed into the lorry waiting to take them away. They would not have been smiling and laughing had they known they had been found guilty and were facing long hard jail sentences. They had been dancing to the tune of the US army, but the end of the song had been deliberately kept from them until they were safely back in a non-public controlled environment, where they could not protest the inappropriate harshness of their sentences.

The White Hart Hotel in Launceston (Shutterstock)

TWO

Spy Centre

When walking North Cornwall's cliffs near Bude it is impossible not to notice the huge array of satellite dishes perched on the cliffs to the north of Bude in the parish of Morwenstow. I wonder how many visitors and holiday makers realise that what they are looking at is GCHQ Bude which is infact one of Britain's main intelligence gathering centres, and is an offshoot of GCHQ Cheltenham. This satellite ground station and eavesdropping centre is located on the site of the World War Two RAF Station known as RAF Cleave, which locals used to refer to as Cleave Camp, and which is the name many still use today.

The construction of the satellite interception station began in 1969, and from the start was a joint UK/US cooperative project. The US National Security Agency (NSA) paid for the major part of the technology and infrastructure, and the running costs were paid by GCHQ which also provided the land. The intelligence collected was, and is, processed jointly and shared by the two agencies. In 2010 the NSA contributed £15.5 million to GCHQ for improvements and redevelopments to the site.

GCHQ Bude has twenty-one satellite antennas (dishes) of various sizes, including three that have diameters of one hundred feet. One of the antenna is capable of receiving signals from thirty five satellites at the same time.

Staff at the Bude GCHQ/NSA station come from both the UK and the US and the facility operates under a formal agreement between the two countries to provide data for the ECHELON signals intelligence network (SIG INT). There are similar stations operated by the West in the US, Japan, Australia, Puerto Rico and New Zealand.

At times concerns have been expressed by the EU and others that GCHQ is intercepting civillian traffic and conducting industrial esopionage. The activities at GCHQ Bude are shrouded in secrecy but in the past investigations by the media including the Guardian, BBC Two Horizon, and Channel 4 have tried to lift the veil.

GCHQ Bude is playing its part in keeping the United Kingdom safe from all sorts of threats and challenges, and will need to continually develop to keep pace not only with enemy and competing nations, but with terrorists, international criminals and others.

Photograph Richard Peirce

Views of Cleave Camp, Morwenstow – Photographs Richard Peirce

THREE

Under the Beach

GCHQ Bude is not the only reason for the Bude area's stratregic importance, and indeed for the strategic importance of other places along the North Cornish Coast. Because Britain is a collection of islands its communications considerations are very different to, for example, countries in the EU which can normally reach each other by surface road or rail. Britain has to rely on air, sea, and undersea for its trade, travel, and communications, and undersea cables are a major element in the country's communications capabilities.

I suspect very few people happily surfing and splashing in the waves on Crooklets Beach in Bude and Widemouth Bay, a few miles along the same coast, realise that under the beaches they are playing on are cables that go out to sea, and are vital for the UK's communications. The whole planet's internet is linked by cables that go under seas, and undersea cables are much more difficult to guard and keep safe from attack than cables on land. The Bude GCHQ spy station is only a few miles away from the cables, and this allows data on these cables to be continually monitored and intercepted.

Look west out to sea from either Bude or Widemouth and apart from the headlands in the south, all you see is sea, and more sea, there is nothing but water all the way to North America, which is why Cornwall is the perfect place for these cables to come ashore. The gently sloping beaches at

Widemouth and Crooklets in Bude are perfect in every way, and give this part of North Cornwall great strategic importance. The first transatlantic submarine cables landed at Widemouth in 1963, and is now where many other cables land and link Britain with the world.

The cable which comes in on Crooklets Beach is Google's Grace Hopper cable which landed in Bude in 2021, is just under 4000 miles long, and is made up of sixteen fibre pairs connecting Bude to New York.

On September 26th 2022 the Nord Stream gas pipeline was blown up off Denmark in three separate places at depths of between 121 and 255 feet. The West thought that Russia might be responsible, but later evidence from German sources indicated that Ukranian saboteurs might have carried out the attacks. What is certain is that this act, and several other undersea explosions, illustrate the vulnerability of such installations many miles from land. International waters are very difficult to monitor, and navies couldn't possibly deploy enough ships to patrol and protect the world's undersea communications cables, which gives island nations like Britain cause for particular concern.

Crooklets Beach Bude - Photograph Richard Peirce

FOUR

The Railway Secret?

In March 1963 a report was published by Dr. Richard Beeching which decided the fate of over 2,363 railway stations and 5000 miles of track. The report led to the closure of many stations and the decommissioning of hundreds of miles of track.

For some reason the track from Taunton to Minehead in Somerset remained in place and was maintained despite no trains running along it for many years. One night in the late 1960's I was having a drink with Captain John Davison, my father-in-law, at the Wellington Hotel in Minehead. We were at the bar and were listening to three or four locals sitting at a table behind us who were speculating why the track was being maintained when no trains were using it?

The conversation obviously amused and interested John so we continued listening in silence. We left before the others and on the way home he told me an interesting story. Not without some authority he explained that the line had been left down and was being maintained for a specific secret strategic reason. After retiring from the army he was appointed catering director at the Minehead Butlins holiday camp. He told me that Butlins was the reason for the track being left down and maintained. He claimed to know that the reason for this was that in the event of war, and civillians having to be evacuated quickly from cities, Butlins could instantly accommodate over 10,000 people. He believed that on top of the Butlin's capacity Minehead's hotels and guest houses could take another 5000 evacuees. Taunton was and is on the mainline from all over the UK, and the Minehead branchline would be vital if a large number of people and stores needed moving quickly.

He spoke as if he knew this rather than was expounding a theory, and given the international situation at the time perhaps his knowledge or his educated guess was correct. Many in Britain still had a Second World War mentality, the Cold Was was at its height and Britons lived with the constant threat of nuclear attack. Many remembered the London Blitz and the evacuations it caused, so who can say that at a time when nuclear bunkers were built all across the country that the "Minehead Rail Plan" might not have been a planning reality, or at least something that was under consideration?

Photograph – Richard Peirce

Minehead Station – Photographs Richard Peirce

FIVE

Shark Suicide Bomber

The account that follows is not a secret but has been largely lost in the mists of time. It is the story of the day a shark blew up the Royal Navy, and I suspect the Royal Navy would have liked the incident to have been kept secret!

The West Briton and Royal Cornwall Gazette dated August 2nd 1956 contains an account of a coroner's inquest at Falmouth. This investigated how two Royal Navy men were severely injured, and two civilians killed, when an attempt to kill a shark by using explosives went tragically wrong.

"Lt. Commander J.W. Bailey explained to the Coroner Mr L.J. Carlyon what had happened when he was in charge of a team of divers working off Porthkerris Point. His colleague Lt. Commander Brooks was working on *HMS Burley* while the divers were operating from a smaller fishing vessel manned by civilians.

Two divers were under water while a third was swimming on the surface. Brooks saw a shark approaching which he judged to be a dangerous animal rather than the 'harmless' Basking sharks that were commonly encountered. Brooks stated that he had experience of sharks in America, so presumably his judgment that this was a dangerous shark was based on that experience.

He saw the shark swim towards the man on the surface. The West Briton newspaper reports 'As it made its run in it turned on its side, which the witness understood was to get its mouth in position to attack. As it came up to the person on the surface, who was unaware of its approach, bubbles came up from one of the divers below. This frightened the shark which broke off its attack and went away'.

The next day at 1.15 pm the *Burley* was back in the same place and so was the supporting fishing vessel. *Burley* signalled the fishing vessel that diving should commence and the divers began putting on their gear. As the divers were preparing Lt. Commander Brooks noticed a shark circling the fishing vessel.

The events of the day before were still fresh in everyone's minds and Brooks sensed there was some anxiety about making the dive.
(NB – Although I believe it is highly likely that the shark/s concerned were in fact Basking sharks we must remember that Brooks and his men were convinced this was a dangerous predator. It is not spelt out anywhere, but one gets the feeling that they thought the shark was a Great White. The events that followed must be viewed in the context that those on the spot were convinced they were dealing with a dangerous animal).

There was a dinghy moored astern of the fishing vessel and the civilians Leslie Nye and his friend Richard Kirby together with Lt. Commander Brooks jumped into the dinghy and set off after the shark with the intention of destroying it. Brooks apparently felt that it was his duty to do this to ensure the safety of his men as he was convinced that the day before the shark had been about to attack the man on the surface.

The account in the report continues..... 'As far as we can tell at this stage, they got themselves right up close to the shark which was near the surface and swimming away from them. They had made two charges to straddle the shark, and together Brooks and Spicer threw them at the shark.

It was a very good shot. A line linking the two charges straddled the shark and got around either its dorsal fin or its tail. The two charges were hanging either side of the shark with the fuses burning. The boat started to turn away from the shark, but the shark turned around and made for the boat, and was underneath, directly aft, when the two charges exploded'.
(*NB – This is the first time in the newspaper account that we hear of the man named Spicer who was also aboard the dinghy).*
The explosion killed the two civilians Leslie Nye and Richard Kirkby, and the two Royal Naval men, Lt. Commander Brooks and Petty Officer Spicer, were both seriously injured.

The estimated time between the fuses being lit and the explosion was 10-12 seconds, and the explosive was 14 ounces of TNT. The court examined whether Brooks had used the right amount of explosive and whether his actions had been appropriate. Lt. Commander Bailey was in the wardroom of the *Burley* having lunch at the time of the explosion. He told the court that he had been told nothing about the dangerous shark being in the area, and thought that diving operations were proceeding as normal. He heard two explosions very close together and thought it was an emergency signal. He went straight on deck where a sailor said, "There is a small boat just blown up".

The small fishing vessel rushed to where the explosion had occurred and was later joined by *HMS Burley*, which had been at anchor and taken longer to get under way.

As soon as the fishing vessel reached the accident location five men leapt into the water to assist survivors. The bodies were taken aboard the fishing boat which steamed at speed to Porthkerris steps. An eyewitness said that the dinghy had been "absolutely smashed to pieces" and he didn't see any sign of the shark.

The coroner commented that it had turned out to be a rather costly experiment. To which Lt. Commander Bailey replied "The whole question of dealing with sharks is very difficult. I spoke to Brooks about it, and he said he was once in an American submarine which got some wires around its screws, and while he and another diver went over the side the Americans held them off with a machine-gun type of weapon".

The report continued.... 'Witness said he understood sharks sensed when the prey they were going to attack was frightened and it was going to be an easy kill, and that when they smelt blood, they lost all fear. On the previous day the man on the surface probably looked likely prey whereas the men in diving suits would appear strange. He believed it was accepted among divers that if they released a few bubbles and shouted, sharks would go away'.

The coroner asked Lt. Commander Bailey whether he would have permitted the use of explosives had he known they were going to be used. Bailey responded that he would have wanted to be fully briefed but he trusted Brooks and his judgment one hundred percent.

Another witness was Leading Seaman P.H. Alderton who was one of the naval divers aboard the fishing vessel. He told how he and Leading Seaman Lusty were preparing to dive when someone noticed a shark circling their boat. He confirmed that Brooks had identified the shark as a 'dangerous type', and that everyone was slightly nervous about diving. Alderton further confirmed that it had been Brooks' plan to go after the shark and scare it away with the explosives. Alderton told the court of the double explosion and said he turned to see pieces of the dinghy flying through the air about two hundred yards away from them.

A helicopter was despatched from RNAS Culdrose to Porthkerris with naval Doctor Surg. Lt. A.C. Johanssen aboard. Leslie Nye's death was due to head injuries and Kirby died of blood loss. It was stated that Lt. Commander Brooks and P.O. Spicer were both still very ill in hospital but were progressing well".

And what of the shark? Was this the first ever shark suicide bomber or did the animal survive? Although Commander Brooks thought this was a predatory shark, I suspect it actually was a Basking shark. These are large animals and blowing one up would certainly result in a lot of blood and shark debris at the site of the explosion. However, the fishing vessel was on the spot in minutes and there are no reports of a live, dead or injured shark being seen.

The Basking sharks I see of Cornwall commonly range between 4 and 6 metres in length. Had this even been a Great White, Mako, or Porbeagle shark of say 2-3 metres, it is still strange there was no evidence if the shark was blown up.

The incident was big news in the area and the explosion occurred quite close to land. So had shark parts been washed up there would certainly have been press reports – I have looked and found nothing.

SIX

Secretive Cats?

There are few animals more secretive than some of the big cat species. I have spent many years in Africa and one of the reasons it is such a treat to see leopards is that sightings are often rare, because they are very good at not being seen unless they want to be. Like many small boys who are fascinated by dangerous predators I have never grown up, and in my case sharks and big cats have been lifelong interests.

At various times in the last few decades there have been claimed sightings of big cats in Devon, Cornwall, Somerset and elsewhere. After a spate of claimed sightings in the early 1980's my cousin Anthony Bush, who was a journalist, was asked by the editor of the Country Landowners Association magazine to research the whole question of whether big cats existed in the wild in Britain. Anthony was a hard bitten journalist who certainly wouldn't believe in monsters, beasts, UFO's or aliens unless he found hard proof. My interest in this subject hugely increased when he told me that in his opinion there were large cats living free in Britain's countryside. Devon, Cornwall, and Somerset are the counties in which many of these claimed sightings have occurred. There is nothing secret about them and indeed they were usually well publicised, however what is not publicised is that many claim that aspects of some of these stories have been deliberately hushed up at government level.

In December 1976 the government's "Wild Animal Act" laid down new measures which would apply to keeping dangerous wild animals as pets in homes. Many big cat owners could not afford the cages and enclosures which were now required by law, and released their animals into wild areas like Dartmoor and Exmoor. Anthony believed this was the reason for the big cat sightings.

I recently came across a film on Amazon called "Panthera Britannica - Declassified" which chronicles the claimed sightings of large cats in Britain, debates the credibility of the stories, and examines whether large cats could exist in Britain living largely undetected side by side with humans. What follows is a list of the sightings mentioned in the film. No 'Top Secrets' revealed, but if they are living among us the cats are doing so largely in secret, and as stated previously there are many who believe some evidence has been kept under wraps.

My own view is that the evidence of large cats being present in our countryside is compelling, and the likelihood is that they were, and maybe still are, doing so in secret and were escapees or animals that were released. Are they breeding, do we have a small population of large cats living wild? I personally doubt it.

Date	**Location**	**Sighting Details**
1790's	Bodmin	A group of French prisoners of war who were housed in Bodmin Jail had been on an excursion outside the jail and on their return reported they had seen a large leopard sized cat. The cat was captured the next day by the army and brought back to the jail where it was locked up. Years later a large cat's skull was discovered in the jail together with a letter written by one of the French prisoners which detailed the story.

26/2/1903	Newton Abbot	A linx killed two dogs near Newton Abbot and was shot by a local man, Mr Heller. Investigations revealed the cat was probably an escaped pet which had learned to live in the wild.
1980	Scottish Highlands	A mountain lion was captured by farmer Ted Noble who had been losing livestock. The cat was sent to the Highland Wildlife Park where it lived until 1985 when it died. Proof positive of a large cat living wild and free in Great Britain.
1994	Banchory Scotland	Alison Parfit when cycling near Banchory came across a large leopard sized black cat in the road and retreated and made a seven mile detour. At the time Alison was also aware of livestock being killed and the remains of a deer being seen hanging in a tree.
1983	Exmoor	There were several reported sightings of a large black leopard sized cat, accompanied by numerous instances of livestock being killed by an obviously large predator. Both the Devon and Somerset police forces were involved in the hunt for the animal. A farmer called Eric Ley lost several sheep, and in the film he recalls how the Royal Marines from Plymouth were deployed to help find the cat due to there having been more than 100 cases of livestock slaughter. At one point a marine rifleman shot at a large black cat from a hide and thereafter there were no further sightings.

		Many assumed that the cat had been hit and died, but no evidence was found to support this.
1983	Barnstaple	A Barnstaple butcher was known to be keeping two large cats as pets for security reasons. One animal was black and the other tawny brown. Apparently it was the butcher's practice to take his cats onto Exmoor to give them some freedom. The man got into trouble with the police and left the county at exactly the same time as Exmoor's black cat was being sighted. The assumption was that prior to running from the law he released the animals onto Exmoor.
1992/3/4	Bodmin Moor	A decade after the Exmoor big cat claims similar attacks on livestock occurred on Bodmin Moor. At the time Paul Tyler (now Lord Tyler) was the local MP, and in the film he recalls being approached by the local Police and the NFU to instigate an investigation. After 12 months the report by The Ministry of Agriculture did not conclude that there was a big cat in the area, but did conclude that there was no proof that there wasn't one!
Nov. 1993	Devon	Police Sergeant Simon Chapman was in charge of a police call centre when a call came through from a man claiming to have released a big cat outside Torquay. A day later a woman called the police to report

		having seen a big black cat near Newton Abbot.
2006	Nr. Plymouth	Dartmoor Zoo owner Benjamin Mee saw a large puma near his zoo. Mee has stated that he knew that the zoo's previous owner had released three pumas, a male and two females, onto Dartmoor.
Dec. 1995	Dunster Somerset	Alex Bowler and Bob Burnell reported seeing a black panther on the Brendon Hills while driving home to Taunton from Dunster.
Jan. 2016	Wiveliscombe	Mathew Everett from Dragonfly Films sees a large black cat in the road near Wiveliscombe.
June 5th 2017	Crowcombe	A mother and daughter out walking on the Quantock Hills came across a large black cat which they thought was a panther. The photos taken by the mother do show a large black leopard sized cat-like animal.
2021	Bossington Exmoor	David Broadley-Doyle reported several sightings of a large black cat in his garden.

NB – The last four separately listed sightings are all clustered in a relatively small area.

2016	Dartmoor	Trailcam footage from cameras set by Matt Jones on Dartmoor captured an image which was identified as being a leopard like animal.
2017	Nr. Plymouth	Dartmoor Zoo owner Benjamin Mee reported that a linx had escaped. The cat

killed at least four sheep before being recaptured weeks later in a live trap.

The film examines the scientific evidence of big cat sightings including DNA results from a hair sample collected from a barbed wire fence near a livestock kill, conclusions from the various pieces of photographic evidence, analysis of toothmarks left on prey victims, and expert opinion on tracks found. The evidence is compelling, from time to time in the Westcountry and other areas it seems big cats have lived wild in our countryside.

Well what do you think? If you ever come across a large wild cat what will you do? Keep it a secret, or report it?

A view onto Exmoor – Photograph Richard Peirce

Dartmoor – Photograph Shutterstock

Bodmin Moor – Photograph Shutterstock

SEVEN

Secret Nuclear Bunkers

Nuclear bunkers are scattered widely throughout the Westcountry. When the Second World War ended with the two atomic bombs being dropped on Japan, governments all over the world had to face and plan for the new destructive realities of weapons of mass destruction. In the years that followed the war it became apparent that for the first time in the history of human development humankind had now developed the means of its own total destruction.

At the end of WW2 the United States, Great Britain and Russia (Soviet Union) were allies. However, soon after the surrender of Germany in 1945 the alliance started to fray before falling apart altogether. With the Soviet Union and its allies (the East) on one side, and the US, UK and Western Europe (the West) on the other an Iron Curtain came down across Europe. A Cold War began which was not waged on battlefields but on economic, political, espionage and propoganda fronts. The Cold War was marked by a nuclear arms race which gave rise to the acronym known as MAD (Mutually Assured Destruction), and was characterised by fierce competition between the intelligence agencies. The Western agencies led by the CIA and SIS (M16) fought their daily battles in the shadows against the KGB (Soviet Intelligence) and its allies.

To counter the threat of Soviet nuclear attack Britan developed its own nuclear weapons, and built a range of facilities including command bunkers, nuclear shelters, and observation posts manned by the Royal Observer Corps. Many of these facilities were underground and enveloped in one metre thick concrete, because it was hoped this would be enough to enable them to survive near misses by nuclear bombs. All over Britain observation posts were set up to warn of an impending attack by Soviet bombers.

At the time these facilities were all Top Secret and public access was almost completely denied.

This chapter is not in any way intended to be a guide to Devon and Cornwall's secret nuclear bunkers, or to provide a comprehensive list. I have picked out some of the places where installions survive to this day.

The Veryan Bunker near the Southwest coast path on the Roseland Peninsula near the cliffs at Nare Head is one of Cornwall's few remaining Cold War posts. The bunker was built in 1963 when the threat of nuclear attack was a daily reality under which Britons lived. This is only one example of a Veryan bunker of which 1,600 were scattered across the whole country.

Lizard Ales are brewed in an old nuclear bunker situated at Pednavounder on the Lizard Peninsula. The metre thick concrete walls and other features make this unused building ideal for the peaceful pursuit of making beer which is a far cry from the building's original purpose. The bunker was once part of RAF Treleaver, and it seems that no pictures of Treleaver still exist.

At the height of the Cold War a secret nuclear bunker was built under the Torquay Magistrates Court. The concrete structure was equipped with very heavy steel black doors designed to help the bunker survive nuclear attack. This bunker had toilets, kitchens, heating and water so was clearly able to be used as living quarters for long periods of time. The bunker was offered for sale in 2018 for £500,000.

The Hope Cove bunker near Kingsbridge was originally a WW2 radar station. It was modified in 1952 into a bunker capable of surviving in a nuclear attack. This Cold War bunker is a listed structure and was put up for auction in 2021 when it made £435,000. The Hope Cove bunker is considered one of the best examples still existing of a nuclear bunker. The RAF left the bunker in 1958 when it was taken over by the Home Office for use as a regional seat of government for the Southwest in the event of nuclear war.

In a sealed area of the Devonport naval base was a nuclear bunker which, when it was recently opened up, was found to still contain written material to be handed out to the public in the event of a nuclear attack. It is thought that this bunker was still in use as a Civil Defense command facility until the early 1970's.

Kilkhampton's Nuclear Bunker

Driving north out of Kilkhampton on the A39 towards Clovelly and Bideford after about a mile there is a large layby on the left. Over the hedge in the field next to the layby is a small area which is largely overgrown by brambles and is fenced off by concrete posts. In the centre of the area a concrete structure can be seen. The structure is the entrance to what was a secret underground nuclear bunker which was active in the Cold War but hasn't been used for many years.

As I write this in late 2023 the shadow of nuclear war has once again fallen over Europe. Since the Russian invasion of Ukraine President Putin has rattled his nuclear sword on several occasions. I can't help but wonder whether in the almost unthinkable event of a nuclear war, Britain in the Cold War was much better equipped to at least partially survive than the country is today!

Bunker in field beside A39 near Kilkhampton – Photographs Richard Peirce

EIGHT

A Dark Secret from Devon's Past

The area that was once known as Exhibition Field is now part of Stanhope Park and Stanhope Close in Holsworthy, Devon. Few users of the sports field and children's playground in Stanhope Park, or those who live in Stanhope Close today, will be aware of the dark secret that hangs over their homes and the park. From 1942 – 1948 the area contained Camp 42, a prisoner of war camp, which housed first Italian, and then German prisoners of war.

The prison camp opened in October 1942 with the arrival of more than 750 Italian prisoners. The Italian and later the German prisoners were put to work on surrounding farms and other projects where labour was short due to the local men being away fighting in the conflict. The Second World War ended in 1945 but it wasn't until 1948 that the last prisoners left Camp 42.

An intriguing fact is that out of the peak number of 400,000 German POW's present in the UK at the height of the war, around 25,000 chose to stay in Britain and start new peaceful lives. Notable among those who stayed in the area after the war was Ted Hemmerle who was born in Freiburg in Germany. Ted was working in France as an electrician with AEG before volunteering for the Luftwaffe. He hadn't been in the air force long before he was shot down in Belgium, became a prisoner of war and ended up in Camp 42 in Holsworthy. During his time as a prisoner he worked outside the camp, as did many others, and when out working he met and fell in love with a girl from the nearby Cornish town of Bude.

Ted returned to Germany with his young wife to start his post war life, but both his father and brother had been killed in the war and his sister was getting on with her life, so after a short while the Hemmerles returned to Cornwall, where Ted eventually went to work for an electrical contractor called Woolacotts. After a period of rapid expansion Woolacotts went bankrupt in 1976, and Ted bought the shops in Bude and Launceston. Ted was very successful and by the time of his death in 2020 Woolacotts had nine branches in Devon and Cornwall and employed 180 people. The German work ethic stayed with him all his life, and Ted was still working until the day before he died aged 95.

1942 – 1948 POW Camp *Housing estate on old camp site*

Photographs Shutterstock

NINE

Exercise Tiger

Exercise Tiger was a rehearsal for the Normandy landings which happened off South Devon in late April 1944. In the midst of the exercise off Slapton Sands German S-Boats, (also known as -E Boats), attacked in an attempt to disrupt preparations for the Allied invasion of Europe. The landing craft that were part of Convoy T-4 were slow and unwieldly, and were easy prey for the German fast torpedo boats.

Exercise Tiger was planned to be as realistic as possible, and so involved men with all their combat equipment, and the landing craft were also loaded with equipment to be used in storming the beaches. Despite the secrecy German Intelligence was aware of the exercise and was watching every move.

The men of Convoy T-4 were to have only two naval escorts providing their defense, but in the event there was only one which was *HMS Azalea*. It was recognised that so many vessels concentrated in a relatively small area was extremely dangerous in terms of attack from the sea or air and so radio silence was ordered. Due to their excellent intelligence the German High Command was not only fully aware of the purpose of the exercise it was also aware of its large scale.

In the middle of the night of April 27/28th British radar spotted S(E) Boats in the vicinity of Convoy T4 however no defensive actions were taken and the convoy was attacked by the Germans. The attacks resulted in at least 749 American servicemen losing their lives. The Normandy invasion was imminent and so the attack incident was subject to strict secrecy, and when news of it did leak out reporting was only minimal. The rehearsal was for the landing at the real Utah Beach which was designated one of the beaches the US Army would land on and is why the casualties were almost entirely American servicemen.

It is little wonder that the incident was as hushed up as possible. It is thought that the eventual death toll was close to 1000, and this was the largest loss of American lives since Pearl Harbour. History would eventually record that it was a higher death toll than would actually happen when Utah Beach was stormed on D-Day.

Exercise Tiger on Slapton Sands – Photograph Shutterstock

TEN

Devon's Secretly Trained Teenage Killers

In 1940 Operation Sea Lion, which was Hitler's plan to invade Britain, would have seen the German 6th Army landing at Lyme Regis. Britain's wartime leaders and intelligence services had seen how unprepared the countries of mainland Europe had been in terms of having organised resistance ready to confront the German occupiers. Had the cross channel German invasion gone ahead Britain was much better prepared to offer effective resistance. Special top secret units, including both male and female teenage assassins were trained and lay ready all over the country waiting to become active in the event of invasion. Those involved in the secret units had all signed the Official Secrets Act which in wartime Britain was perhaps adhered to more strictly than it is today. Someone aged 15 in 1940 would have been in their mid 90's by 2020, and it seems that Britain's teenage secret agents have taken their secrets to their graves with them.

The existence of the Home Guard/Dad's Army is well documented, but that there was also a top secret army of teenage boys and girls trained to kill only recently came into the public domain when a book by historian Andrew Chatterton was published. Chatterton's book for the first time exposed how boys and girls between 12 and 16 were trained to kill Nazis using various weapons including knives, garottes and firearms.

From the summer of 1940 MI6 set up the secret units in six counties and Devon was one of them.

The teenagers were trained to be snipers, wireless operators and assassins. These units were a million miles from Captain Mainwaring's Dad's Army. The young people were highly motivated, ruthless, trained secret agents lying hidden and waiting in British society. Wireless sets, weapons and other equipment was hidden in Devon's churches, pubs and other places, and sometimes whole families were recruited. Chatterton's book is called *Britain's Secret Defences: Civilian Saboteurs, Spies and Assassins During the Second World War*, and he exposes in detail how Section VII would operate should an invasion occur. The children were trained as if they were adults by army NCO's who were in uniform but with all insignia removed. As well as how to kill they were trained in all the other aspects of spy craft that would ensure their effectiveness and, hopefully, their survival. Sabotage, dead letter drops, wireless operation, and secret messaging were among the skills taught to Britain's secret teenage assassins.

The operation to train the young people seems to have been beyond 'Top Secret', it could almost be called ultra Top Secret, and this may have been because the powers that be did not want it to leak out that Britain was a country which was ready to use children as killer agents.

ELEVEN

Devon's Secret WW2 Heroine

Agent Rose was also known as Mademoiselle du Tort, Alice Wood, and Jacqueline Duterte, but to her family she was known as Didi. Agent Rose's real name was Eileen Nearne and she died penniless and alone, apart from her cat, in a small flat in Torquay's Lisbourne Crescent. It was only when Torbay Council officials searched her flat looking for details of any next of kin that they discovered details of her astonishing secret wartime life. Eileen Nearne would have been given a council paid funeral and what was once known as a pauper's grave. However, when the news became public her death made headlines around the world, and she was given a guard of honour at her funeral which was attended by representatives from all three of Britain's armed forces, as well as the Military Attache and the Consul General from the French Embassy.

During the war she had served as a radio operator with the codename Rose, and had been part of the Special Operations Executive (SOE) for which she was parachuted into occupied France on several occasions. She was captured three times by the Nazis, and each time held out against her interrogators before escaping. After the war she was awarded an MBE by a grateful British government and the Croix de Guerre by the French.

Three years after her death Prince (now King) Charles unveiled a monument to her and other female wartime secret agents at RAF Tempsford in Bedfordshire. Sir John Sawers, who was head of MI6 (SIS) at that time, praised the extraordinary bravery of the female agents who had helped ensure the Allied victory.

Eileen was born in London in 1921 and was hand picked for secret service as an agent. She was one of three children born to an English father and a Spanish mother, and both her siblings also became SOE operatives.

After the war she lived in London with her sister and it is thought she moved to Torquay sometime around 1990. She was found dead in her flat on September 2nd 2010 after neighbours became concerned. She never spoke of her wartime past to any of her neighbours in Torquay and so took her secret wartime life to the grave with her. Her funeral was attended by her niece Odile who is believed to have been her only surviving relative.

Eileen Nearne – Photograph Shutterstock

TWELVE

Secret Junior Warriors

Secret Submarine Attackers

Both the British and German navies started making use of submarines in the First World War. The German submarines were known as U-Boats and the German navy started deploying them increasingly from 1915. Little did they know that in North Cornwall they would face a secret force of small schoolboys. Arthur Madge was from farming stock and was North Cornwall born and bred. Aged about seven Arthur started attending a private prep school in Bude called St. Petroc's. Activities included long walks along the cliff tops in the Bude area. War broke out in 1914 when Arthur was six or seven, and a couple of years later on calm days German U-Boats started using little bays and inlets on North Cornwall's sparsely populated coast as places to surface and run their engines to charge their batteries. They hadn't bargained on the St. Petroc's Junior Home Guard!

Sometime in the 1990's I met Arthur at his sister's house in Crooklets in Bude, and he told me how on one school cliff top walk he and the other boys had looked down on a high tide and seen a German U-Boat on the surface in a little cove. The boys had wasted no time in gathering stones, bricks and anything else they could find to throw over the cliff at the vessel. Whether they hit the boat I don't know, and certainly this junior artillery barrage would not have altered the course of the war. But I am sure that this would have been one defense response the German Naval High Command wasn't expecting. Arthur died in 2016 aged 108.

A German Spy? Arrested in Bude

Some 24 years after Arthur Madge and his St. Petroc's prep school friends were raining missiles onto German U-Boats recharging their batteries in coves beneath the cliffs around Bude, seven-year-old Len Tozer and his spy hunting gang were busy at work around Bude looking for enemy agents in World War Two.

Len's father had died soon after he was born and his mother supported herself and her son running a guest house at 31 Victoria Road in Bude.

Len cannot remember exactly how events unfolded but he does remember that the older boys in the little gang were always on the lookout for spies, and that his friends talked about seeing a person/s signalling out to sea from Bude's clifftops. He is not sure whether the older boys reported their suspicions to the police. However, he does connect one of those staying in his mother's guest house with being a suspected German spy.

His mother kept a visitors book which Len still has, and he believes that Susanne Saunders (see picture) from Falmouth was a suspected German Secret Agent. The boy's suspicions were added to when on June 30th 1940 Police Constable A.K. Ware (P.C. 158) came to his mother's guest house, arrested Susanne, and took her away. Len does not know what happened to her and strangely, for a small town, the rumour mill was silent. Had the boys identified a German spy, or was Susanne arrested for some other reason?

The answer may remain lost forever in the confusion of war, but what is fact is that she was arrested and then disappeared never to be seen or heard of again.

Left - Guesthouse in Victoria Road
Below – Guesthouse Entry made by Susanne Saunders

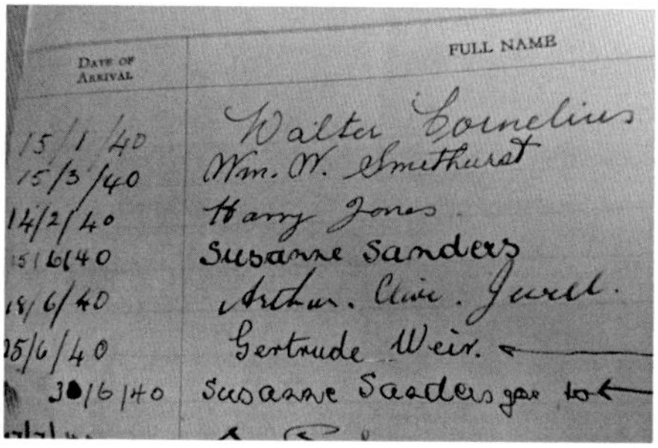

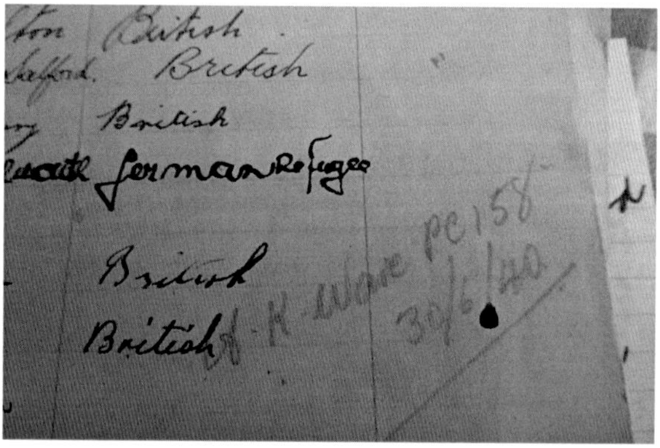

Guestbook Entry made by PC A.K. Ware – Photographs Richard Peirce

THIRTEEN

Secret Snippets

The Real Jamaica Inn?

Some years ago when I was writing my book *Execution Sites* I interviewed the then owners of the Red Post Inn which lies between Holsworthy and Bude on the A3072. The reason the Red Post Inn was of interest for that book was that Red Post was once a place where hangings were carried out.

The pub owners told me an interesting tale about a theory that their pub was the real location and inspiration for Daphe Du Maurier's *Jamaica Inn* story. They claimed that they had records of Du Maurier staying there, and that many aspects of the story fitted the Red Post area better than Bodmin Moor. Whether they had any proof I didn't know, but they believed that Du Maurier's publishers had been instrumental in the decision to base the story on Bodmin Moor rather than North Cornwall, because they thought that an inn on a well-known tourist route would sell more books than one in a more obscure area. After hearing their theory I quickly skip re-read *Jamaica Inn,* and found there certainly are aspects of the book which belong as much in the Red Post Inn area as where the story is now set. In the 18th and 19th centuries wrecking and smuggling were rife on the North Cornish Coast, and the Red Post Inn was a known centre for these activities.

Irrespective of whether the Jamaica Inn claims are true or not Red Post has its secrets. There was a false chimney in what is now Red Post Cottage which had a secret room built into it for smugglers to hide their contraband. A gallows stood at the nearby Red Post crossroads, and it is believed that the last public hanging which took place on the site was in the mid 1800s for sheep stealing.

Top: The Red Post Signpost
Above: Red Post Cottage (The Old Red Post Inn) – Photographs Richard Peirce

Paying Tax

When we moved from Bude to Exeter, as is normal in moves, we cleared a lot of stuff out. Then, as is also normal, I kept coming across things that I wanted but had taken to the skip. One of the things that made a one-way journey to the skip was a Cornish magazine, maybe *Cornwall Today*, which had a fascinating article in it talking about old Cornish laws which had never been repealed and so were theoretically still valid.

One such law was relevant to the paying of taxes by Cornish people. The article claimed that there was still a law in place which said that Cornish people only had to pay taxes to the Central Exchequer (London) if the Duke of Cornwall approved such a payment. I always wanted to write a letter ….. "Dear Chancellor, I am sorry but I am withholding my income tax payments this year until the Duke of Cornwall has informed me I should pay them"! I planned to cite the old law, and send the letter to the papers as well as the Chancellor. I wish I had.

Cornish Independence

Cornwall has its own language, once had its own parliament and has its own flag. The river Tamar's source is less that three miles from the North Cornwall coast near Morwenstow and it flows into the sea in Plymouth Sound. For much of the river's length it forms the border between Devon and Cornwall which means there is water between Cornwall and England for several miles.

In recent times there were efforts to revise the Cornish Parliament based on the fact that many old laws, including the 1508 Charter of Pardon, still existed which gave the Cornish rights of self determination. This was taken seriously enough for questions to be raised in the House of Commons where, sadly, for the Cornish claims for more independence were denied.

The President (To Be) Returns

One of the Royal Navy's most decorated WW2 units were sailors based in the Dart estuary in South Devon who roared back and forth across the channel delivering secret agents to Nazi occupied France and bringing home aircrews which had been shot down.

The naval unit named the 15th Flotilla was very special indeed, it had to be to evade the German E-Boats which patrolled the channel ceaselessly seeking to destroy them.

No one could have known it at the time, but in February 1944 one of the boats speeding across the channel was taking a young Frenchman home. A young Francois Mitterrand, later President of France, was stationed in Kingswear during the war as was General de Gaulle's son, Phillipe. By the end of WW2 the 15th Motor Gun Boat Flotilla had made more than 100 high speed dashes to and from occupied France, and those involved were awarded more medals than any other Royal Naval unit.

Secret Guinea Pigs

A previously secret UK government report commented on in The Guardian in 2002 officially confirmed that between 1940 – 1979 the Porton Down Research Establishment carried out secret tests on the UK's population which involved biological weapons and which the public were not told about. The tests were to help the MoD to assess the vulnerability of the UK population to biological attack from the Russians. In most cases alternatives to biological weapons were used which the scientists believed were harmless but would mimic biological weapons. The report reveals that 'Fluorescent Particle' trials between 1955 and 1963 involved dropping huge amounts of zinc cadmium sulphide on populated areas from Northeast England to the tip of Cornwall.

Between 1961 and 1968 from Torquay to the New Forest over a million people were exposed to the Anthrax imitating bacteria E.Coli and Bacillus Globigii. (These were two examples of the secret mass testing which occurred, and which may still be going on). In 2002 Sue Ellison, a Porton Down spokeswoman, was asked whether such testing still continued, her reply was "It is not our policy to discuss ongoing research"!

Photographs Shutterstock

FOURTEEN

No Secrets

Devon and Cornwall have the highest concentration of nudist beaches anywhere in the United Kingdom. Although not a secret, that is not a well-known fact, and the naturist enthusiasts certainly would like to keep the bare-all areas as secret as possible. There are no physical secrets among those who have shed their clothes at these locations. Perhaps surprising however is that many of these beaches are quite well-known.

It is reported that use of nudist beaches is on the increase, and apparently those who accidentally stumble across unexpected bare flesh don't stare, they either tend to look away or simply retrace their steps and leave, and there appears to be very little peeking and voyeurism.

Some of the following nudist beaches are officially registered as such and others are not. So as not to blow the lid off completely and expose all I am only listing general locations and not publishing a map.

- Pedn Vounder Cornwall
- Budleigh Salterton Devon
- Slapton Sands Devon
- Perran Sands Cornwall
- Basset's Cove Cornwall
- Downderry Cornwall
- Fishing Cove Cornwall

-	Great Perhaver	Cornwall
-	Penhale Sands	Cornwall
-	Porthmeor Cove	Cornwall
-	The Strangles	Cornwall
-	Bovisand Bay	Devon
-	Western Mouth	Devon
-	Wild Pear Beach	Devon

Several years ago, I wrote a magazine piece about naturists (nudists) and can remember parts of the interview I did with one of the 'bare all' fans who explained her rationale for stripping off as follows. "We are all born naked, when we die we no longer need clothes, so it is only in the middle bit that clothes are sometimes needed for protection against the elements or for showing off". She believed that as long as you are warm enough, not being burnt by the sun, and not wanting to show off, then the only reason to wear clothes is to satisfy what she saw as society's small-mindedness. She was also convinced that nudity promoted honesty among individuals because having no physical secrets encouraged frank and open social relationships. I asked if people ever joined nudist places for voyeurism and titillation, she thought this definitely happened but, with a slight smile on her face, said she felt sorry for men who were not genuine because if they got excited it couldn't be hidden, and a man would be laughed at. She also believed that very few men were as impressive as they thought they were! Having explained this, she made clear that she thought that non-genuine naturists were rare.

Wild Pear Beach Devon – Photograph Shutterstock

Perran Sands Cornwall – Photograph Shutterstock

Bassetts Cove Cornwall – Photograph Shutterstock

Budleigh Salterton Devon- Photograph Shutterstock